Ron Kipling Williams

Black
Freak
Mosh
Heaven

Black
Freak
Mosh
Heaven

Ron Kipling Williams

Brother From Another Planet Press
Baltimore, MD
ronkiplingwilliams@gmail.com

For those who hug the world

Table of Contents

I don't care what people believe. All I care about is they love all people they can see, and not just the god they cannot.

Pray for the dead, and fight like hell for the living.

Mary "Mother" Jones

All the freaky people make the beauty of the world.

Michael Franti

Am I Who?

i doc martin ancient stomps to the ground
punching rage machine against the hollow lament
of minions who stagger follow the greedy age

megaphone my chromosomes to the bomb spits
hits insanity blasts sane pressing on humanity

i want to bail out so i can persevere over more bailouts
brilliant volcanoes mix factory artistry my art history
tired of labeled "BEST KEPT SECRET"
roses don't fuck with me when I am dead

since 10 i have been processing addict food
jamming throat down shit to cope with more shit jams

crash—die—diet—crash—rash—diet

cycles more vicious than washers of old industrial
high fructose corn syrup banging more than Pop Iggy
crammed neon yellow and red into colons like
McDonalds, Wendy's, and Burger King

knowing better enough to be old and
foolish young to fuck up again this world
needs to come into me better so i can make it
but orgasms come of war, not love

my dreadlocks lock–out the fire–brain
childhood days i see through window–pain
hopes like ropes that keep me hanging
walls like drywall to keep me banging

cemeteries of buried people bell ringing
with no bell wishing i can unbury them

being only left wing or right wing
leaves a chicken running grungy circles

middle fish swimming mainstream
makes happiness stream claustrophobic
and putting God into a lock box
within a church box has
locked God out

border breaking breaks borders broken
and leaping fences leaps over mending
wounds never mend when borders never
break broken fences always mend leaping

an unlocked car is the safest place for safe keeping

radical like chemical reactions
free radicals my radical sabbatical
is in your face

my black–red dread rolls like
a rock and roll head phone
human rights rolling roving
loving being human

Sometimes
You Want to Give Up
Your Flesh

I'll never forget the time when I went to see one of my all time favorite bands, Killing Joke. It was at a small venue in Fells Point in Baltimore. I looked across the room and saw the only other black guy in the place. We caught each others' eyes, and we nodded, like it was some kind of code or something.

There is no box.

Black Freak Mosh Heaven

black boy

in black gear
in nail bracelets
in doc martin boots

inside
he flails about
in the mosh pit
in sweat
in gritted teeth
tribal screams of
angst

outside
hyenas across the street
hoot and cackle
call him a freak

fuels fire through
his veins
like an electric
adrenaline shot

Bad Brains
Nine Inch Nails
Dead Kennedys
Ministry

hell freaking
yeah

he
mixes it up
with other bodies
seeking
to feed
the angst

warrior clashing
carrying tribal
ritual
raising ancient
spirits
emancipating
the shackled
dead
freeing
lost souls

in the
beautiful chaos
bodies
jump off speakers
fallen bodies
picked off the floor
and thrown
back in
the fray

muscle memory
takes over as he
hits the wall

becomes
smeared
black on black projectile
as he gets
second wind

he and his
mosh comrades
morph into a profuse
sweaty stinky
mess

hell freaking
yeah

lights go up

he left everything
in the pit

he will do it again
next week

inside
the tribe of freaks
rejoice

outside
steam hollering from
his head

he stretches his arms
to the Great Spirit
and feels buffalo blood
coursing through his veins
stomps djembe drums
on the ground
as Chango marrows
his bones

his punk rock
body
and cultural soul
synthesized

West of the Park

I grew up in DC
on the other side of 16th Street
in Rock Creek Park.

I was lucky to be born
on the 'right side' of 16th Street.
That was the claim of
Midwest–born white reporters
on the evening news.

I did not have to cook meals
for my younger siblings,
or fight off drug dealers and pimps,
or work after school
for my clothes and shoes.

My light skin
and proper manners
were cute in the eyes of
the blue haired ladies
in the consignment shops
and the soccer moms in the mall.

My backpacked
Catholic school body
was never bruised by
a PR–24 control police baton
or handcuff clamped
or shoved into a squad unit.

When crack flooded the city,
I rode down Georgia Avenue
in my parents' town car
and saw dark–skinned men
pinned over automobiles,
their nostrils on fire.

When my voice deepened
and my limbs lengthened…

Suddenly,
their urge to touch my cheek
and pat my shoulder stopped.

Suddenly,
16th street blended both sides into a cage
where I was lumped in with the boys
on the other side of the divide on Cops.

Suddenly,
I heard sounds of locking doors
and clenched purses
and whispers to cross the street.

Now,
nothing guarantees my safe passage,
not a Ferrari, not a Mumbai mansion,
not a top–level security clearance.

There are those in the white community
who tell me to get over it,
but they do not try to walk in my shoes.

They only tell me,
that my goal should be to position myself,
to land once again on the right side of 16th Street
and serve hors d'oeuvres.

Clipped

My father
took my
moustache.

I was 15
and proud of the
fuzzy peach—

I was becoming a man.

It was at Kiski,

a private summer school
architectured on the lush hills
of Saltsburg, PA

where at lunch
I was commanded
by the headmaster
to cut my sandwiches.

One day,
the headmaster told me
my moustache must go.

I said, hell no.
He said, then I will call your father.

I was ushered into
a plush oak study room
where the old guard
poised inside antique frames.

I was backboned straight,
confident that my father
would come to my defense.

My father, who as a boy
jumped the segregated fence

in Northeast Washington, DC
with his friends,

beat up the white boys
and jumped back over
before retaliation.

The headmaster
spoke minutes into my
father's phone ear.

After my moustache
was erased from my face,
the headmaster patted me on my back.

That day my hero,
the scrappy kid
from Northeast DC
melted through the
phone line,

casting me into
a darkness where identity
is crushed like brandy ice
below the frames
of ancient masters.

I have grieved ever since
that I could not one day
sit with my father

and laugh about
our scrappiness together.

Body

I have been
                    flogged
                            about
                                    my body

since I was born.

Since I can remember
the marauders

scorched
my nerve endings

on a timer.

My body
sought asylum.

Blubber
like yellow spray foam
insulated
my body

red dots
peppered it.

Even if
            I possessed
the head of Medusa

could I begin to be vindicated?

psychic
damage
trumps
arsenic.

To me Hostess Ho–Hos was like junk food caviar. The treat was contained in a white wrapping with a tantalizing photo. Inside were two cylindrical chocolate mounds filled with heavenly white cream, gently resting upon a rectangle of cardboard. But my mom and dad would never let me eat junk food in the house, and certainly not before dinner time. I had to eat a well–balanced meal, followed by a dessert of which they approved.

One day when I was 13 years old I succumbed to my Hostess Ho–Hos craving. I rode to the store, made my purchase and proceeded toward home. But wait…where to eat it? I decided the alley that curved behind our house would be my dining spot. I stopped the bike, pulled out my Hostess Ho–Hos and began devouring them. So there I was, resting on my bike, ravaging my Hostess Ho–Hos, and whose vehicle pulls up behind me?

My father's.

I looked up. My father's face morphed into a scowl. He barked for me to get in the house. I cannot remember exactly what happened next, but I imagine he gave me another one of his infamous two hour lectures on being responsible, for which there was no rebuttal. I was to sit there in shame, with my esteem crushed, and two Hostess Ho–Hos churning in my belly.

Jah Hannibal

as if a car suddenly collided
with your body
and you are flung in the air
then bounced on
the asphalt pavement

the night I received
the text about Jah Hannibal

i held myself together
i thought

for the next few days
everything felt like…

i should have talked to him more

i should not have been so selfish

it was my fault

he told me one day
as I talked with him on my cell
walking toward Lexington Market
that he needed more conversations
like ours

we traveled to Frederick
to play drums at a show

he told me
sometimes you just want to give up
your flesh

in the midst of our usual
political conversations
i thought it was another one of his
deep statements
and I gave him a 'mm–hm'

like a soulful call and response

on the morning of
may 7, 2012
he gave up his flesh

13 days later
at the memorial celebration

i gave up my tears

it took two consoling loved ones
for me to gather together
and play my drum
and tribute my poem

meanwhile
in his truck
in that last place of
earthly sanctuary
before his
last exit

Jah Hannibal
did something for us
for his closure
and our healing

that morning
he wrote a poem
thanking us
for the years
we were with him
he asked us not to mourn
but to celebrate his life
for his journey here
was over

that first line
which haunts me
with bittersweet tones
reads as follows…

it's a beautiful day

my champ

I.

every weekday morning
when i was five years old,
i would lean in the second floor
brown shuttered window
in our san francisco home
and watch my father
dressed in a dark suit and briefcase
stroll up the hill to work

in the evening,
i would rush to the door
to greet him in his work smell
leap into his arms
and upon his lips
kiss my champ

every day
like our sturdy backyard tree
i climbed up his
pedestal
crafted by my heart
and squeezed him

he was a six foot oak
a half octave voice above
James Earl Jones,
a brown and thick
Sir Walter Raleigh,
dashingly handsome,
clean cut, polished,
and smooth

he was everything
a sapling could aspire to be
if that sapling
would ever be

II.

one night,
when i was eight,
i nested in my father's lap
in our new home
in Washington, DC

we watched a movie
called the champ

in the movie,
after a brutal boxing match
the champ lay dying,
his limp body on a table
in his dressing room
smelling of sweat
and age

his son, little t.j.,
leaned over his father's
puffed and bloodied face,

he pleaded
for his champ
to get up

but his father died,
leaving little t.j.
alone

bawling,
shaking,
i confessed to my father
i was terrified he
would abandon me

my father
engulfed me in his breast

as if I was a cub
his lullaby voice promised me
that he would
never

III.

as I left his lap
and began to explore
my own path

his bark boiled
at my adventures

but he also feared
I may never be
that sapling off
the oak tree

IV.

when i was 15
a maple seed drifted
from the neighbor's yard
into ours
and sprung two leaves

my father and i
cradled the seedling
and planted it

by then
our bond had cracked

my innocence shed
revealing a new skin of
rebellion and self–discovery

it was repulsive
to my father and foreign
to the one he had made
for me

yet we committed
to this seedling
to show that something
could grow in our
home

two decades later
was the last time
my father and I witnessed
the seedling that grew
into a maple tree

the pedestal
I made for him finally
collapsed
and one october day
we parted ways

V.

within months
i returned to the cracked home
he left for san francisco
plastered, painted, and placed
with new owners

smiling crushed and empty
i panned the new furnishings
chatting with friendly strangers

with their permission
i toured their home
soaking in memories

i revisited my seedling
as a matured maple
a hollow victory for me
reuniting with my tree

i know nothing
about right decisions
i know
my champ is long gone
and my sage whiskers
bear its burden's brunt

i know
in the corner of
spider web moments
i am bawling, shaking
little t.j.
waiting
to climb into his lap
waiting
to feel his reassuring breast
waiting
to gaze upon his stride
and to leap
and kiss him

and to sit
in the sturdy backyard tree

and wait
for another maple seedling

Broken Legacy

I feel like a tourist
whenever people elaborate on their family tree,
and when I hear about family reunions,
I'm a nomad in a land of clans.

I have Blackfoot, Seneca,
and Cherokee in my family.
Most are dead.
some disavowed their heritage
to pass for white or black.

My paternal great grandfather
passed for black. He worked
as a Pullman porter on the railroad.

My material grandmother
passed for white, so she lived
as a white woman.

These are all the stories I have.

I was never taken to a reservation.
I was never told my people's history.
I have no artifacts or trinkets.
I have nothing to pass on.

My family branches
are broken, the trunk fallen
and split, and the roots are
overgrown. I have learned
to bury my pain and move on.

I live as an American black,
with all the rights my African
ancestors fought and died for.

I have no idea who they are.
No stories. No artifacts. No records.
Nothing.

I feel like a tourist
whenever people elaborate on their family tree,
and when I hear about family reunions,
I'm a nomad in a land of clans.

Tracks opened in 1984. It was the biggest gay nightclub in Washington, DC in the 80's and 90's. It was located south of Capitol Hill, in a huge warehouse building. It had one massive dance floor with a performance stage area, a smaller one with a video screen, a deck and pool, an outside bar and grill, a beach volleyball court, an outside dance floor—oh yeah, and a popcorn machine! The biggest feature about it was its atmosphere. It was a judge free zone. Everybody was accepted, and just about every social group hung out there—punks, Goths, alternatives, metal heads, skate heads, hip hop heads, reggae heads, jocks, princesses, the business crowd, jarheads, preppies, yuppies—you name it, they were there. You didn't see guys pumping their testosterone in the air, nor did you see women throwing cat eyes, or fighting outside the club. You definitely didn't have to worry about somebody cutting or shooting anyone. You could dance by yourself and nobody thought you were weird. In fact, a lot of people did, and it was totally cool. You saw all kinds of dancing there, from moshing to ballet. There was everything from spikes to suits, from gowns to grunge. Everyone was allowed to be free and be themselves. For a lot of us it was a sanctuary, away from the judgments and cruelty from the mainstream world. When it closed down in 1999, it was truly an end of an era. There will never be another club like it. Thank you Marty Chernoff for all the great memories. You created a place that many of us called home.

Blessed are the Radicals

Tolerance is the arrogance of the ignorant.

Angry

"You are an angry man,"
she said.

In my East Baltimore neighborhood,
the bus is rarely on time during rush hour,
and often rolls by because it is full.
Commuters from the county enjoy
punctual trains and buses.

21 years after his anti–crime bill,
Bill Clinton said he was wrong.

The prison population has doubled since then,
and now the industry publicly trades on Wall Street.
Thousands of families have crumbled on the front stoop.

When I was living in Arlington, Virginia,
I was pulled over because my muffler was loose.
The police patted me down and searched my car,

asked me if I had any drugs or weapons,
asked me why I had a spoon that smelled like
peanut butter in my glove compartment,
asked me why I had paper in my backpack
all because I had a loose muffler.

Officer Daniel Pantaleo
killed Eric Garner by putting him
in a chokehold and holding him down.

The medical examiner
ruled his death a homicide.
Pantaleo was not indicted.

"You're cool for a black guy. You're
not like one of them," my George Mason
University dorm mates declared.
They danced and grunted like monkeys,
mocking black guys from "the ghetto."

Baltimore city school administrators
enjoy heat and air in their offices,
while down the hallway students
freeze and boil, and eat cardboard food while
administrators enjoy delicious take–out,

and because MTA buses refused to board students
at Mondawmin Mall on April 27, 2015,
students took pieces of crumbling buildings and threw them.

In the aftermath of the financial crisis of 2008,
Thousands of Americans lost their homes, jobs, and businesses.
Wall Street bankers avoided jail and parachuted into millions.

I was one of my Corporate branch's top employees,
Then I got injured. My doctor gave me light duty.
Corporate refused. I went on short term disability.

It expired. I had to resign because I was still hurt.
Corporate blocked me from unemployment compensation.
I consulted an attorney. He told me Maryland is
an At–Will state. I didn't have a chance.

While Flint, Michigan residents went bankrupt buying bottled water
and watched their children suffer with lead poisoning,
the water company threatened to cut off their contaminated water
if they didn't pay their bill.

For 15 days in October 2013,
Congress shut down the government.
The millionaire elected officials got paid.
Their paycheck to paycheck employees didn't.

Iran. 1953.
Congo. 1965.
Cambodia. 1969.
Chile. 1973.
Afghanistan. 2001.
Iraq. 2003.

Libya. 2011.
Haiti—

One day I wore a scarf on the job.
My boss called me Aunt Jemima.

Another day he and his co–workers
were standing around my desk.
"They have Black History month, Women's
History month, everyone else gets a month—
what about white man's month?"

A black historian once criticized
Thurgood Marshall's serious face in photographs.
He never received Thurgood's death threats,
or had to travel in a coffin to escape detection from the Klan.

But, like she did,
the black historian had to be put in Thurgood's shoes.

Then I turned to her and said,
"Apology accepted."

In My Neighborhood

In my neighborhood,
a man was running
from two pit bulls

                                        he and a car
                                    did not see each
                                               other

the car
lifted from the
asphalt
and slammed him.

I heard the police
helicopter
and stepped outside.

                                        Beyond the
                                    yellow police tape

the paramedics
were pumping his chest.

I saw his shoes.

Officers removed
One of the pit bulls crouched in a
backyard.

                                A woman hustled toward
                                            The scene

"Please God
let it not be him!"

She made a phone call
then scampered away to go to
the hospital.

                                        On one corner
                                    neighbors huddled

"The police need to
put   them   dogs   down!"

Figuring nobody called the news,
I called FOX 45.

A reporter came on the scene.

On the news that night,
they reported the incident.

Gov. O'Malley signed a bill
passed by the State Assembly

making it difficult
for victims of pit bull attacks
to sue their owners.

Swerve this,

Fuck   poetry.

Those green digits
that ticker along Wall Street screens
is America's wordsmith.

We are pork bellies,
posing as artists.

Today's Caesar,
parading fruit loins
                              in
                                        London. Milan. Paris.

The runway
is window dressing.

Vomit
oozing from garbage compactors
adjacent to/two day old
knife–gut–rot–bodies
are the pen and paper,

fall
from chewed/up squats
above drug stashes
in planter boxes,

twist
two legged snakes
cracked up in smoke
strolling someone else's baby
for trade.

lift
Florida fruit pickers
to jerry rig flea markets
from dirt and dead grass.
We   sweat-boil/font–push
whore's gold on trade paperbacks.

*We have come to a point in our society
where art serves more as commodity
than as community.*

For Trayvon

I was walking home
when Jim Crow leapt upon my back
and ripped out my spinal cord
and devoured my flesh

They identified me by dental records
and in the days following
I reanimated into a national headline
just for walking home

Profanity is what you see every day.
Words don't do it justice.

Blood Minerals

Shantytowns
no running water
no electricity
miners lose sleep

for pennies
slaving
to deliver stones
stones shipped
shaved and cut
glimmer from pruned hands
at the Met
bounce on high walker
fashion ways
fitted on wedding
ceremony days

AngloGold
Anglo American
Anglo cold
on black tears
lungs black
apartheid is back

Cecil Rhodes
Rothschild
DeBeers
JP Morgan

pneumonia
silicosis
phthisis

Witwatersrand 1946
violence on union miners
at their doorsteps
for their silence
no compunction
for conspicuous consumption

shopping mall sheep
flock to blood mineral
for cheap   er   prices
We the beef eaters

flee from the knowledge
of how cows are
slaughtered

capital punishment
in miners shafts
one cough at a time
the American sheep
never sit behind the glass

Black velvet boxes
resting under Christmas trees
above dirt
above dirt
above dirt
below the other side
of the earth
pine oil boxes
resting under wailing knees

No eulogy
for sooted black on
cracked black hands
mine fruit pickers

'there will always be poor people'

blood flows
from shipping boxes
to merchandise windows

minerals lost forever

Tear Drop

Brianna
denies the laser
that could eliminate
the tear drop on her face

She believes
she dropped too many tiers
to rise out of the game

Brianna
is a junkie of the daddy kind
whose love only responds
to the money she brings

She always returns
to her man
who sends her into the night
to allow the sharks to feed

The gutter
does not hold Brianna's fall
the sewer water underneath
becomes a resting place

Meanwhile
the steel underbelly
of the city corrodes
and the subterranean
dwellers fester

A shark bears his teeth
as city steam
shrouds Brianna's
pummeling

The street bounces her body
and a manhole cover
tattoos her defeated skin

Brianna's broken teeth
lie on the asphalt of
crushed dreams

Brianna's future omitted
from the daily column
toe tags are cinematic
if the story sells

cold cases boil
in heartbroken families
who rub photographs
and grind carpets
and overheat car engines

the prodigal tear drop
prayed over saline soaked
bible pages

no milk carton photos
or press conferences
when a tear drop
falls too many tiers

only door knocks
and fallen knees
and cries for Jesus
and escorts to the morgue

the next full moon
daddy casts his looming eyes
and with his catcher's mitt
lands a new
tear drop

I was told I would grow up once I ceased monotony spitting about black wrists and ankles in shackled chattel past/the battle conquered is on the mantle/picturesque as Dr. Kings' dream

I was told I would become mature when I stopped feet stomping about Native Americans bear–trapped on blood–soaked plains (this land is "our" land/love it or leave it and it will always be the Washington Redskins, prairie boy)

I was told I would be a refined adult when I shred my race card leap the color blind hurdle and get over "it"/to the victor go entitlements/get your hands off my manifest destiny!

According to politicallycorrect.com, our great nation no longer strikes through black names on job applications. They are only scored for polish. (Tamika and Jaquan, by the way, are names that lack polish)

A red pickup truck hurled 'nigger' at me at 20mph. I was in a part of town where I dared not ask him to slow down.

I infantile thrash about the floor/child bitch smash in the toy store/my teeth gnashing bashing at brown and black droopy silence around the clear water cooler as blue bloods victim slam, Michael, Eric, Freddy/the suspect is described as a male black/who else runs with a hoody?

I used to believe that retail staff who took my potential purchases to the front counter were providing excellent customer service until I noticed they weren't doing it to anyone white.

I was sitting at a restaurant when a waitress asked me if I didn't mind moving from my table at the front window to one near the kitchen. She nervously smiled and said, "You know?"

During a heated conversation over race I was having with a dorm mate at my first college I asked if he thought black people were inferior. He replied, "You're getting better."

"We the People" blossom as mature citizens when we whitewash the ugly truth and bleach the dark genocide into something that appears 'long, long ago in a galaxy far, far away'

My rite of passage is to chuck the bullhorn and the picket sign/soften my voice/raise my right hand over my chest and pledge allegiance to the dry eraser

Another long hot summer comes where bombs and bullets fly/more blue–white knuckles bruise blue-black flesh…and mature black people file into church/eye beg white Jesus in stain glass/and sit on their hands

Bullet Dodging

In urban America
there is no debate over
drugs   and   guns

The natives do know
in front of   plywood windows
and   garbage collages

both are in trade

to take a life
is about
money
and territory
and business
and respect
on the bus
alleged assassins munch on their cell phones
about upcoming court dates
and plea deals

30 years ago
they could not   point
on a map
where Iran   sits

the Contras and Sandinista
sounded like a Spanish dances

and wasn't Somoza
a drink?

They
never processed poppy seeds
or cocoa leaves

or stuffed duffle bags
or military coffins
or third world tummies

Before the 11:00 news
Mama's family is dumbfounded
by brilliant crazy white suburbanites
who shoot up schools and movie theaters

Mama says
a series of good ass whippings
would have prevented Columbine
and Aurora
and Newtown

The next day
she will stand behind yellow police tape
gripping a bible
wondering
when she spared the rod

wondering
where has the neighborhood gone

wondering
why the mayor only comes during election year

wondering
why
the deaths of black and brown people never make
ABC, CBS, NBC or Fox News
unless it is a riot

Perhaps
a bullet needs to hit
the right tax bracket
the right zip code
the right voting district

Mama's neighborhood
is shot in sepia tones on the local news
with a Wild West soundtrack

Meanwhile
on Dateline
'Adagio for Strings'
crescendo as tear strewn faces proliferate
a Torn suburbia

across America
Mothers' knees
dig into carpets every night

Praying   for safety
signal   failure   is   optional

Georgia Peaches

I.

Today

Two people are dead
Martina and Troy

brother and sister

Martina,
hoped she would predecease

Troy

But the Georgia State Parole Board
had different ideas

7 out of 9 recanted testimonies
didn't matter

YOU
don't matter   Troy
You
WILL die

echoed through courthouse walls
collapsed appeals
upon the book of   justice
Martina
prayed it would turn a new page
just   once

But for Troy
who was in the wrong   place
at the wrong   time
with the wrong   skin
only needles
only needles

II.

I
who mourn for   Troy
mourn more for my own   loss
than his actual   death

I rage
for again not being heard
being ignored yet
Again

I scream
at the system   flushing
common sense
reason and evidence
down the toilet

I   boil
for America's
smug stance

I weep in   staccato
on the inside
the camel's broken back
rolling back and forth on the floor
as if it were   satiated

Only Troy rests
in his own coffin
I   drained from battle
drained from battle
need
peace

III.

You do the crime   You do the time

is the mantra of many
protected behind walls
and gates and redistricts
and railroad tracks
and invisible boundaries

Martina
her arms and neck of
dark chocolate brown skin
extending elegantly
from a blue shirt that read
I AM TROY DAVIS

She
with a pride of a thousand generations
refused to be moved

Today

Across America
I   who remember
and mourn
cannot eat a   Georgia peach
without the bitterness

Commodity

I.

Adjacent to
Lexington Market
God pimps in uniforms
spits scripture
like black widows
at recovering addicts

II.

ATM machines hum
inside steeples
as oily palms
receive bills
to bestow upon their
pimp's coffers

Apparently
God
who created the
universe
needs cash

III.

God
in white restraints
peers at orderlies
through pane glass

God
scratches hieroglyphics
with a shank
at the federal
penitentiary

God
illustrates on cardboard

under the highway
underpass

God
wipes blood between
legs after daddy leaves

God
fails the high school
standardized test

God
gives blowjobs
in squad cars
after giving up
drug money and
product

God
has food stamps
cut off

God
contracts lead poisoning
from slumlord neglect
and loses court case

God dies
and is buried
in Potter's field

IV.

God is
for sale

Armageddon
has never been more attractive
to those who cannot see
the god within themselves.

for they hug the world,

the Mohawks,
the rude boys,
and the suburbanites,

the cowboys,
the steampunks,
and the neo souls,

the cybergoths,
the tree huggers,
and the aloofs,

the geeks,
the luddities,
and the goths,

the dorks,
the Otakus,
and the groupies,

the hackers,
the cosplayers,
and the bikers,

and the freaks,
the trekkies,
and the Afropunks,

the industrials,
the hipsters,
and the metaphyisicans,

the hippies,
and the nerds,
and the stoics,

the metalheads,

the rock climbers,
and the hip hopers,

and the emos,
and the grunge,
and the bingo players,

the surfers,
the gamers,
and the jugglers,

the jocks,
and the street walkers,
and the traceurs,

the panhandlers,
the preppies,
and the hillbillies,

the divas,
the nomads,
and the trash divers,

the self-talkers,
the jocks,
and the asexuals,

the agnostics,
and the rednecks,
and the swampers,

the blue hairs,
the yuppies,
and the bible thumpers,

the grey hairs,
the hybrids,
and the circus freaks.

Blessed are the radicals
for they see the beauty of
world,

in all its bends,
and twists, and gnarls,
and knots, and scars,
and holes, and
scrapes, and cracks,
and stains, and
tears and rips,

and embraces them all
as perfect imperfections.

So there I was, in the midst of the alternative/gothic/punk/industrial scene, when I got involved in social justice movements. I went from dancing at Tracks and slamming in the mosh pits to shouting, "No Justice, No Peace". It wasn't easy in the beginning. I was still the middle class black kid from Rock Creek Park. I knew nothing about demonstrations, protests, marches, or anything like that. Frankly, I was scared to death of getting arrested. So the first few protests I left when things got heated. But I kept coming back, because I knew something was wrong in this country, and I had to do something.

I don't care what people believe.
All I care about is they love
all people they can see,
and not just the god they cannot.

And Now For Something Completely Trippy

Resonant as bass under Bootsy Collins thumb Afrofuture dreams liberate my song/I was trudging like sludge in the urban Bayou because no one digs a half caste half breed hybrid skybrid universal ahead of his time soul brother/Like Sun Ra I believe space is the place as I crock pot my next intellectual meal to those who are ready to taste/I have become the grape by which those who press are enlightened/ there is no sky in my realm for I punch holes in dark matter and create a form in which I hang as I pluck notes alongside Bootsy's Rubber Band/and I understand we are George's One Nation Under a Groove/ However we are here grasping for intra–terrestrial straws and intergalactic nourishment overlooking the underpinnings of our salvation which is the mechanisms in our innards/the plucking of Bootsy bass continues because he is steady waiting patiently for us to catch up/we are the tomatoes of our destination/will we be the masters or will we be compost/up to the ship we space/will we crash upon the nebulous horrific gate/I am slated to collaborate with my elder cosmic brothers as I transition from flesh to fantastic/the transition begins when I transform my blood to wind

Naked

I.

adam
was ashamed
to be naked
in truth

in the face
of a jesus rant
on a subway stop
i quell my tongue

this gray–bibled
thump muffin
shouts to the bubble dome
of the holy war
between believers
and non–believers

II.

momentarily
i am han solo
in a holy crusade
trash compactor

below me
human remains
for the sake of god

women raped
because it was eve's fault
clinics bombed because
women choose

native people
forced to worship
jesus

whipped out of africans
their drum
their language
their god

III.

my head throbs
as the carousel
of atrocities

i don't care
what people
believe

all I care about
is they love all people
they can see
and not just the
god they cannot

IV.

the self-proclaimed
prophet states

there is only
one god
the god of abraham
the god of isaac
and the god of jacob

those who do not believe
will not be saved

V.

it takes
everything in me

to not give her
the verbal beat down
i think
she deserves

but i won't
give her the satisfaction
of witnessing me
lose control

and not live
what I preach

instead
i collect myself
and walk away

VI.

i believe

we need to stop
thumping our
beliefs on the heads
of those we
need to love

and instead

strip
ourselves down
to be naked in
truth

VII.

i am not adam
i am not ashamed
i embrace truth

Visiting Day

I.

One winter I hung
my identity in the closet
to visit my parents

one more rekindling
to salvage family ties
dripping through cheesecloth.

before them I hunched
inside walls I hallucinated
as penitentiary concrete.

"How are we going to have a
relationship with your hair like that?"
my mother asked.

I felt brillo pad eyes
staring at my skull
as if it was in alien form.

My first inclination
was to exit cordially
and never return.

But my assignment
was to have closure
before death parted us.

They removed the velvet rope
I entered their exclusive club.
I pulled myself taut.

II.

I wonder
how many carcasses
swing from family trees?

How many bodies are
shackled in orange jump suits
at annual reunions?

How many innocents
are gutted and served
at the family feast?

I resolved one day
to remove myself
from their menu.

III.

Autumn four years later,
the last season
I would self mutilate.

I reflect
on my bittersweet liberation
while suturing my wounds.

No longer ancestral drawings
in the caves of my memory
to ground myself.

It is excruciating to sever
parental connections
even for self preservation.

IV.

I know
they loved me hard
and with all their breath.

They who
sacrificed mountains
so I may prosper.

They who
constructed ramps so I
may leap over their backs.

They who
anguished nights over paper
to balance the bottom line.

I will never know
the aches from wearing battle armor
nor the pain from skirmishes

the miles they trudged
the health they jeopardized
the future they augmented

the sorrow that engulfs them now
to be estranged from the one they
once called their pride and joy.

V.

How many children have
jabbed needles like artwork
licked bottles squeaky clean

sucked pipes to the bottom
cast their bodies to fiends
and given up their flesh

because the two people
that encompassed their world
could not stand their sight?

I never knew my grandfather. He abandoned my mother when she was very young. After my mother gave birth to me, he came to visit. I was crying. "Can't you get that baby to shut up?" She told him to leave.

When I was old enough, my mother told me about him, that he was a prominent stage actor in New York in the 50's, 60's and 70's, and appeared in films like *Shaft's Big Score, Don't Play Us Cheap,* and Gordon Parks' *The Learning Tree.*

One day I was going to the Kennedy Center with my good friend Darryl Wharton–Rigby, a filmmaker who was receiving an American Film Institute award. I told my mother about it, and that Ossie Davis, one of our fine American actors, would be there. She told me Mr. Davis knew my grandfather, and to ask him about what he knew.

After the awards show ended I approached Mr. Davis. He was tall and statuesque, a gentle giant. I told him that my mother said he knew my grandfather, and told him his name. Mr. Davis quizzed me about what I knew about him. After satisfying his curiosity, he placed his hand on my arm and said, "Tommy's dead."

I was neither sad nor angry. I did not know him, so I had no strong emotional attachment to him. Yet I felt lost, like yet another part of my history was gone, and I had no connection to it.

I did feel a sense of irony, that Thomas Charles Anderson, who had no desire to know me, had a grandson that would follow in his artistic footsteps.

Love Means

not being afraid of you.

Before?

I,
knee–begged,
panic–bargained,
back–prostrated for walk over,

fool. repeat.

Post cycle,
the mirror
walked away.

The last
post–fool,
my TMJ
placed in front of me
a stop sign.

I refuse to die
from stress.
from you.

It is time to
rebut you.

I am that I am,
so deal,
or don't.

If you hate me,
good.

If you crash and burn,
you'll do it alone.

I've been rummage
long enough.

If you leave,
go.

Take your baggage,
your memories,
your lint balls,
and your air,

so I can bleach
my soul of you.

rainbow saints

candace and shirley
clasped hands   gazed eyes
at their backyard
celebration

finally married
after three decades   plus one year
of battle

with the state
for the right for   same genders
to marry

facial crests of
serene   bitter   joy   lament

I boil at the bones
they did not deserve
31 years   of hurt

My irrational mind
wished it had chicken wire
to cut clean off
the church's head

and stake it
on candace and shirley's deck post
next to the smoker

candace and shirley
the saints   i am not

would have charged me
to put it back

and mend it
with their rainbow

New Human

everyday
i want to be
seen as a
new human

looked upon
as the magic being
that I am

i want you
to look at me

and discard
your usual intake

of my
tackled tanned
skin

as a threat
to you

accept me
as you accept
yourself

shake my hand
and know I am you

new human me
so you can stop
playing those old
tapes

no one
should be subjected
to your fears

Every stranger is a potential friend.

Homage to an Elder

I burrow into
the flesh of an
elder tree

ingest its
heartwood
vibrate its
ancient hums

arms
tunnel through
its branches

legs
plow through
the roots

feet
bathe in the warmth
of mother soil

scalp
tingles from
the breath of
the sky

locks
cling to its bark
like vines

eyes
melt into the folds of
leaves

ears
tune to the
music of bark
I weep in joy
for the magic

of this elder tree
and
offer myself
as an artifact.

The Skin of One Land

All we want
is for a seat
at the table
and to have
a conversation,

a conversation
of what it means to be
a human being
in America.

After all,
the table was made by immigrants
inside the house built by slaves
sitting on top of land wrested from Indians.

I believe
we all are owed at least that.

We know
there was no promise
written on parchment paper
centuries ago

for all of us

but we
living together in this age
in this land
have made that promise
of 'We The People'
to each other.
Every morning
we in a great rush
deliver our children to
school
and ourselves to
work

and though
we blare horns
and swear
and make
obscene gestures

we also in a great rush
lift a car off a citizen
trapped underneath

work for hours
until one is rescued
from a collapsed
coal mine

cover each other
as bullets fly
in a school,
or mosque,
or movie theater.

We arduously debate
our own sacred truths
and our private passions

but our
collective 206 bones
and our
transfused blood
compels us to reconcile
in common squares.

It should be our
imperative
to inaugurate all of our voices
for our national
table conversation

so that each one of us
can move about freely
within our skin

that the world
may see our progress
deeper than skin

and our promise
to each other
yields a new skin

the skin that fits
on one table,
inside one house,
upon one land.

When I was boy, I had a dream of giving the world a hug. I've been through a lot since then, witnessed horrific things, learned about the ugly truth of America and this world. As a result I have been aware and outraged. But I still hold on to my boyhood dream. Even when I am stereotyped, vilified, and cursed just for being who I am, "the other", or when I see people mistreated and abused, I hold on to it. Sometimes, my boyhood dream is all I have to hold on to.

The Dance

my body evaporates
'weirdo, fat boy, redbone'
glued to me
like duct tape

as attention shifts
I am aware
eyes that caress
and sting

I move my flesh
stronger and faster
boot stomping the beat

my head tingles
I spin my body
eyelids massage my soul

my skin
slick and beaded
the monsoon comes
my sweat haunts

I am shaking
rejection from girls
who told me
my hair was too long
and my belly too fat

the woman
with three children
who pointed to me
and said, "bad!"

my father
who stole my
studded belt
and handcuffs
from my closet

and took it to
my psychiatrist

my father
who shouted,
"you must be fucked up!"

the ghetto pterodactyl
who bruised my face
and mugged me

the thieves
who broke into my house
and almost killed me
in my sleep

I shake the haunt
off my back and
flood love back to me
like internal orgasms

as night moon
melts into itself

I feel myself
indivisible
invincible
irresistible

I unlock my power
and float on
tribal notes

I am
superlative,
sublime,
supernatural,
and flesh
that is free.

Love without borders.

About the Author

Ron Kipling Williams uses art, media, performance, activism, education and mentoring to break down walls, facilitate open and honest conversations, and build community. He has appeared on several radio and television programs, and performed and lectured in numerous venues throughout the Mid–Atlantic Region. He won a Maryland State Arts Council Individual Artist Award, a Baltimore City African American Male Unsung Hero Award, and a United Workers Human Rights Champion award. He has a new one man play, Dreadlocks, Rock & Roll and Human Rights. Ron is graduating with an MFA in Creative Writing & Publishing Arts from the University of Baltimore. He volunteers as a voice–over recording artist for the Maryland Library for the Blind and Physically Handicapped.

Acknowledgements

This book is a merging of my experiences and artistry over the years, and my immersion in the MFA program at the University of Baltimore. The poems are a result of three years of struggling, wrestling, persevering and liberation. I hope you enjoyed my literary journey.

Big thanks and gratitude to the Hoffberger Center for Professional Ethics at the University of Baltimore for funding this book. I have been honored to participate as Student Fellow. Dr. Fred Guy, Cindy Myers, you are the best!

I have had an incredible time in the MFA with my professors, and my colleagues—many of whom have become friends. Thank you for your encouragement, support, comraderie, and love.

To my Thesis workshop comrades—Sylvia Fischbach-Braden, Andrew Klein, and Mary Walters who gave me such wonderful support, encouragement and ideas. Thank you for your poetic nurturing.

Thank you Sharea Harris. You have been the sister I never had.

It was Sharea, Tommy Koenig, and Jessica Welch, who brainstormed with me, as I created my one–man show, *Dreadlocks, Rock 'n Roll & Human Rights*, on the whiteboard in the Resource Room at UB. I will always cherish that workshop session Thank you my friends.

To my mentors—Dr. Monique Akassi, Dr. Diedre Badejo, Dr. Fiona Glade, Dr. Lenneal Henderson, and Dr. Myra Waters. I am grateful for the tools, coaching, nurturing, and love that you gave me to reach this point in my journey.

Thank you Kendra Kopelke, Steven Leyva, Stephen Matanle, Meredith Purvis, Pantea Tofangchi and Marion Winik for guiding me through the process, as I opened my creativity and polished the rough edges to come out of it a freer, more focused writer.

Deepest gratitude to my family, the ones who keep me on solid ground —Leilani, Caleb, and my beloved Suzette, who through her patience, support and love uplifted me, challenged me, and believed in me even during the times when I doubted myself.

The book cover and inside pages were designed by
Ron Kipling Williams.

The inside pages main typeface is Adobe Garamond Pro 12pt.
The accent typeface is Futura 24pt.
The size of the book is 8x6.

The cover photo was taken by Laura Melmed
on Friday, July 17, 2015
during the performance of my one–man show,
Dreadlocks, Rock 'n Roll & Human Rights
at the Baltimore Theatre Project
as a part of Artscape, the city's annual arts festival.

The author's photo was taken by
David Sebastiao of Acrosonic Media.

"Blood Minerals", "Georgia Peaches", and "The Skin of One Land"
were previously published in *Poets' America Anthology*.

"Visiting Day" was previously published in *Plorkology: Stories, Poems, and Essays*.

"Homage to an Elder" was previously published in *Skelter*.